CONTENTS

EVERYBODY'S BODY

We follow rules when playing games with friends and learning in the classroom. They keep us safe. Rules can make sure everyone has fun.

LIFE WORKS!

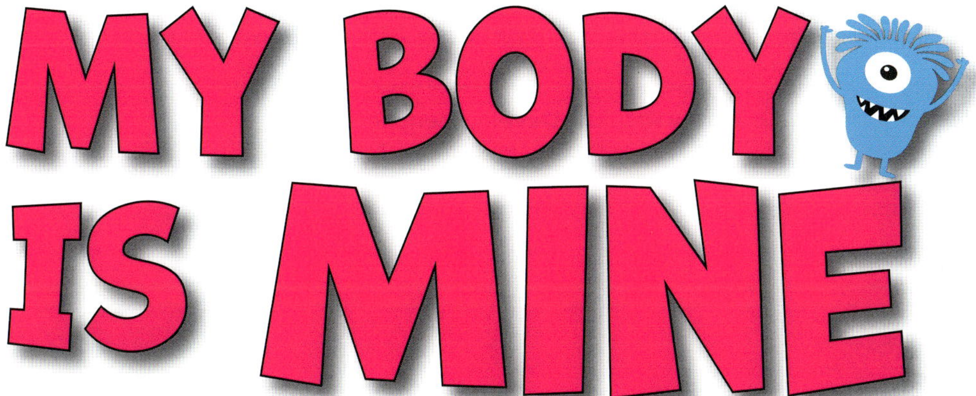

MY BODY IS MINE

HOW TO GIVE AND RECEIVE CONSENT

by Sloane Hughes

Minneapolis, Minnesota

Credits: 4, © Ground Picture/Shutterstock; 6, © Krakenimages.com/Shutterstock; 7T, © Monkey Business Images/Shutterstock; 7BL, © Sklo Studio/Shutterstock; 7BR, © Gelpi/Shutterstock; 8T, © AJP/Shutterstock; 8B, © PeopleImages/iStock; 11, © Neliakott/Shutterstock; 11, © SpicyTruffel/Shutterstock; 12, © monkeybusinessimages/iStock; 13, © PeopleImages/iStock; 17, © LeManna/iStock; 17, © wong sze yuen/Shutterstock; 21, © Inside Creative House/Shutterstock; 22, © Daxiao Productions/Shutterstock; 23L, © PeopleImages/iStock; 23R, © max-kegfire/iStock.

Bearport Publishing Company Product Development Team
President: Jen Jenson; Director of Product Development: Spencer Brinker; Managing Editor: Allison Juda; Associate Editor: Naomi Reich; Senior Designer: Colin O'Dea; Associate Designer: Elena Klinkner; Associate Designer: Kayla Eggert; Product Development Specialist: Anita Stasson

Library of Congress Cataloging-in-Publication Data is available at www.loc.gov or upon request from the publisher.

ISBN: 979-8-88509-963-9 (hardcover)
ISBN: 979-8-88822-140-2 (paperback)
ISBN: 979-8-88822-283-6 (ebook)

For more information, write to Bearport Publishing, 5357 Penn Avenue South, Minneapolis, MN 55419.

We can also make some of our own rules. Each person gets to make choices about what happens to their body.

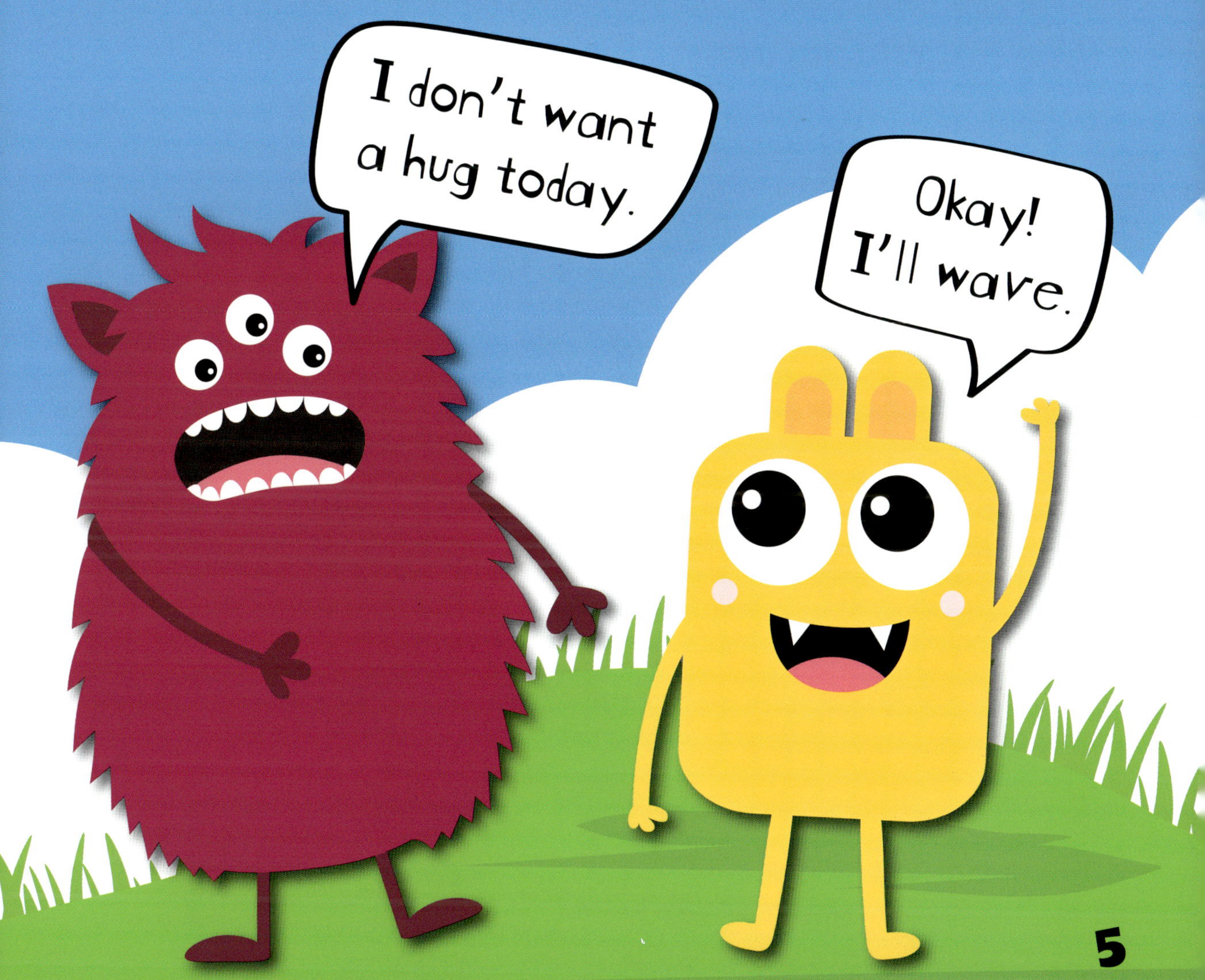

ALL ABOUT BOUNDARIES

Giving **consent** means agreeing to what happens to you. It also means saying no to things that do not make you feel good or safe. We set **boundaries**.

Sometimes, our boundaries are about **physical** space.

We may want only close friends to call us by a nickname.

We can set boundaries about what to talk about.

DIFFERENCES ARE OKAY

We are all different and so are our boundaries. Something that's no problem for one person might be a big deal to someone else.

Thinking about other people's boundaries is important because we all matter. It shows **respect!**

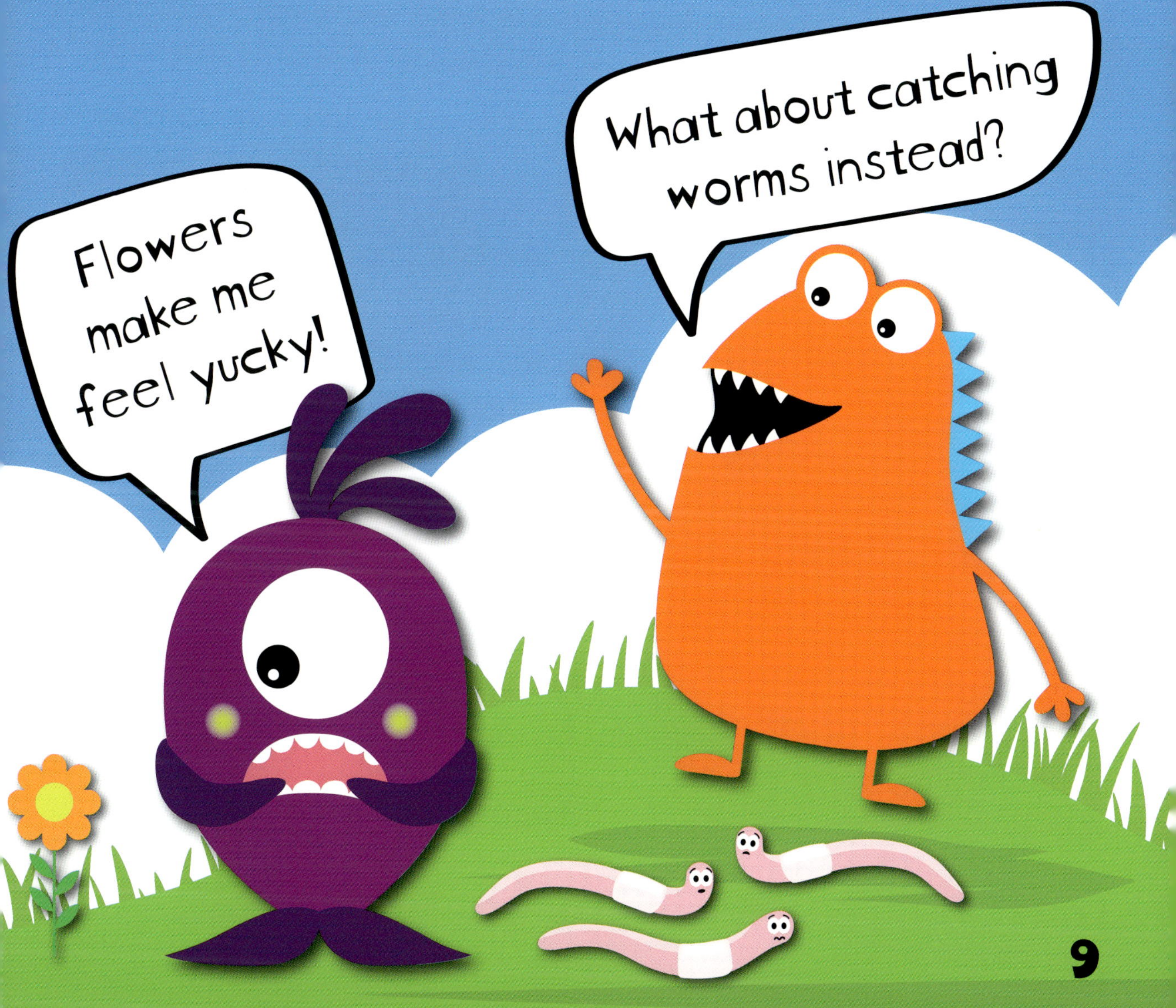

SETTING BOUNDARIES

Make some a-MAZE-ing boundaries with a friend!

1. Gather a group of friends.
2. Grab some pillows, blankets, or other large objects.
3. Then, take turns setting up a maze using your objects.
4. Follow the boundaries to get through the maze.
5. Switch who is in charge of making the maze. The boundaries may change!

Let's set some boundaries!
I'm ready to respect them!

CLEAR COMMUNICATION

How do we set our boundaries? To give consent, we have to **communicate** clearly. When we are okay with something, we can say so.

We also have the power to say no if we do not want something. It is okay to say how we feel!

Sometimes, we need **privacy** to be by ourselves.

SAY GO!

Practice giving the green light go-ahead with a group of friends!

TRY IT:

RED LIGHT, GREEN LIGHT

1. Make start and finish lines.
2. Pick one caller. This person stands at the finish. Everyone else is at the start.
3. When the caller says "Green light!", those at the start can move toward the finish. Everyone must stop when the caller says "Red light!"
4. Anyone moving after "Red light!" needs to go back to the start.
5. Play until someone gets to the finish.

Green light! Go!

ASKING AND LISTENING

Getting consent is just as important as giving it. This means we ask before doing something. Then, we have to listen to make sure it's okay.

It can be hard when someone says no. But we shouldn't do something without consent.

We should get consent before we use someone else's things. Just ask!

LISTEN UP

Practice careful listening in a fun way!

1. Find a group of friends. Pick someone to be Monster.

2. Monster will give commands. Others will listen.

3. If Monster starts the command with "Monster says," do the action. If they don't start like that, do nothing.

4. Listen closely!

5. Take turns listening and being Monster.

Monster says . . .
touch your eyeball!

WHAT ABOUT NOW?

Boundaries can change over time. Just because we were okay with something in the past doesn't mean we need to be okay with it now.

Change is okay! We get to keep giving and taking away consent. And we should keep asking others for theirs, too.

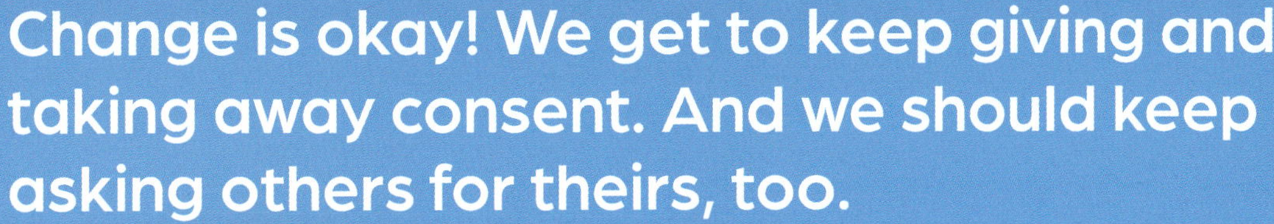

When was the last time you changed your mind? It might have been about consent or something else!

WE'RE IN CHARGE

My body is mine. Your body is yours. We all have a choice and a voice. Consent is cool!

I have boundaries!
My choice is okay!

GLOSSARY

boundaries places and ideas that mark an end or limit

communicate to share information, ideas, feelings, and thoughts

consent approval of or agreement with what is done

physical having to do with the body and other material things

privacy being left alone or given the space to be by oneself

respect a feeling that someone or something is good and important